Y0-AGU-318

Smithsonian

LITTLE EXPLORER

Matter

by Megan Cooley Peterson

PEBBLE
a capstone imprint

Little Explorer is published by Pebble,
1710 Roe Crest Drive, North Mankato, Minnesota 56003
www.capstonepub.com

The name of the Smithsonian Institution and the sunburst logo are registered
trademarks of the Smithsonian Institution. For more information, please
visit www.si.edu.

Library of Congress Cataloging-in-Publication Data
Names: Peterson, Megan Cooley, author.
Title: Matter / by Megan Cooley Peterson. Description: North Mankato, Minnesota :
Pebble, a Capstone imprint, [2020] | Series: Smithsonian little explorer. Little physicist
| Audience: 6–8. | Audience: K to Grade 3. Identifiers: LCCN 2019004949 | ISBN
9781977109620 (hardcover) | ISBN 1977109624 (hardcover) | ISBN 9781977110657 (pbk.)
| ISBN 1977110657 (pbk.) | ISBN 9781977109668 (eBook PDF) | ISBN 1977109667 (eBook
PDF) Subjects: LCSH: Matter—Juvenile literature. | Matter—Properties—Juvenile
literature. Classification: LCC QC173.16 .P48 2020 | DDC 530.4—dc23 LC record available
at https://lccn.loc.gov/2019004949

Editorial Credits
Michelle Parkin, editor; Kyle Grenz, designer; Eric Gohl, media researcher;
Tori Abraham, production specialist

Our very special thanks to Henry D. Winter III, PhD, Astrophysicist, Center for
Astrophysics, Harvard and Smithsonian. Capstone would also like to thank
Kealy Gordon, Product Development Manager, and the following at Smithsonian
Enterprises: Ellen Nanney, Licensing Manager; Brigid Ferraro, Vice President, Education
and Consumer Products; and Carol LeBlanc, Senior Vice President, Education and
Consumer Products.

Image Credits
Science Source: David M. Phillips, 7; Shutterstock: 123dartist, 19 (bottom), Alesia Kan,
4, Alexey Repka, 23 (left), Alta Oosthuizen, 29 (bottom), Anastasiia Craft, 19 (bark),
AR Images, 24, Billion Photos, cover (middle), Chen Peng, 19 (blocks), CHIARI VFX,
cover (top), corbac40, 9, COULANGES, 19 (dolphin), danylyukk1, 27 (inset), Designua,
25, Evannovostro, background (throughout), Evgeny Drablenkov, 14, George Rudy,
21, Jef Wodniack, 5, Jezper, cover (bottom), Jeroen Mikkers, 19 (ducklings), Kuzmenko
Viktoria, 26, Lesterman, 19 (soup), Magdalena Kucova, 12, majivecka, 23 (person),
Olha Yerofieieva, 8, Piotr Piatrouski, 19 (igloo), Sean Locke Photography, 10–11, Serkan
Senturk, 27, snapgalleria, 6, Songchai W, 29 (top), Take Photo, 1, 15, Tarasyuk Igor, 13,
TUM2282, 17 (bottom), udaix, 15 (inset), Unkas Photo, 17 (top), Vadim Sadovski, 23
(planets)

All internet sites appearing in back matter were available and accurate when this book
was sent to press.

Printed in the United States of America.
PA70

Table of Contents

What Is Matter?

Look around you. Everything you see is matter. Your shoes and bed are matter. Even the house you live in is matter. The sun, moon, and stars above you are matter too. Matter is anything that takes up space and has mass. Matter can be a solid, liquid, or gas. It can be soft, hard, dry, wet, bumpy, or smooth.

Human-made objects are matter. Anything that you can build or make is matter.

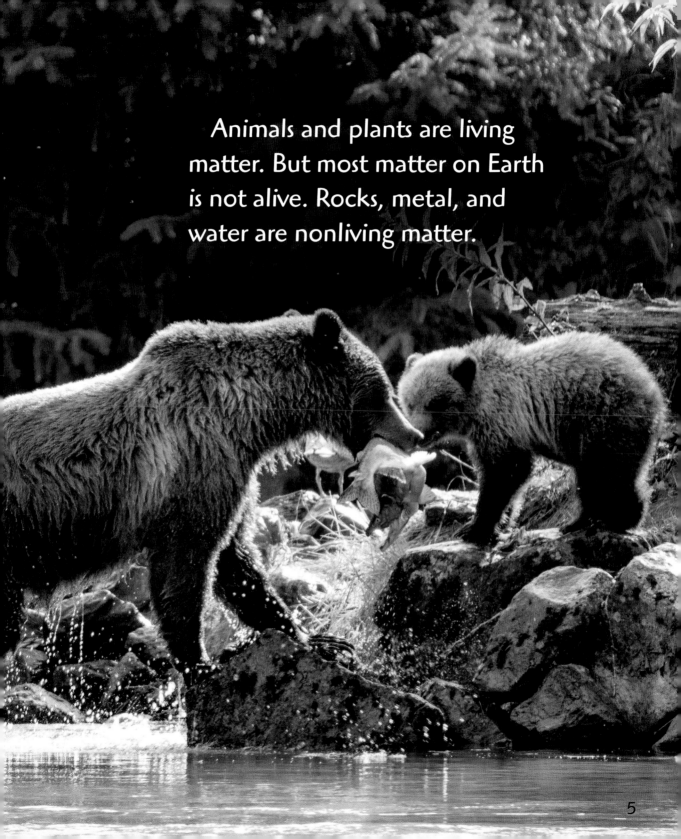

Animals and plants are living matter. But most matter on Earth is not alive. Rocks, metal, and water are nonliving matter.

Building Blocks of Matter

What is matter made of? All matter has atoms. Atoms are too small to see without a microscope. Living things are made of cells. Cells are made of atoms too. The human body has trillions of different kinds of cells. One cell has about 100 trillion atoms.

A single atom is a million times smaller than the width of a human hair.

structure of an atom

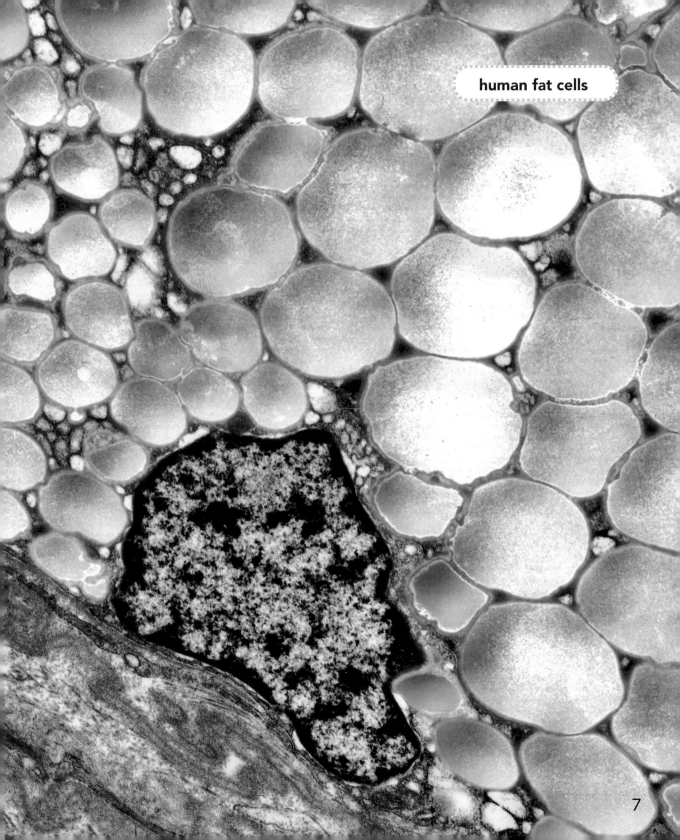

human fat cells

7

States of Matter

Three states of matter are solids, liquids, and gases. Solids hold their shape. Liquids have no shape of their own. Gases constantly change their shape.

Your body is made of all three states of matter. Your bones and muscles are solids. Your blood is liquid. Gases such as oxygen flow through your blood.

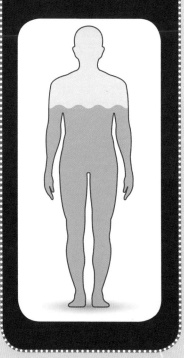

About 60 percent of the human body is made of water.

ice

solid

water

liquid

steam

gas

9

Solids

You use solid matter every day. Your toothbrush, shoes, and backpack are all solid matter. The atoms in a solid object are bunched together. They can't move around. This is how solids keep their shape.

Not all solids act the same. Pull on a rubber band. It stretches. If you let it go, the band goes back to its original shape. Now try to bend a potato chip. It will break in half.

Liquids

Pour water into a glass. The water takes the shape of the glass. What happens if you tip the glass upside down? The water spills out into a puddle on the floor. It doesn't hold its shape like a solid.

Water, oil, and syrup are all liquids.

Liquids have no shape of their own. They take on the shape of whatever they're poured into.

Gases

Gas is another state of matter. The air you breathe is a gas. Air is always bumping up against you. Wave your hand quickly through the air. Can you feel the air hitting your hand?

Gases change their shape. Unlike liquids, gases completely fill whatever they're put into.

You may think that fog is a gas. But it's actually a liquid. Fog is made of tiny water droplets.

The air in a hot-air balloon makes the balloon float.

Gas atoms have a lot of space between them. They can spread out or move closer together.

gas atoms

Most gases are invisible to the human eye.

Materials

Materials are made of matter. Water, soil, and wood are examples of materials. Turn on your faucet. Water pours out. Dig into the soil and plant a seed. Use pieces of wood to build a tree fort.

Humans use materials every day. Cotton can be made into clothing. Logs are burned for heat and light. Glass is used to make windows. Builders use steel to make skyscrapers.

Concrete is a human-made material. People use concrete to build roads, bridges, and buildings.

17

Physical Properties of Matter

Matter has physical properties. A physical property is something that you can see, touch, or smell. Matter can be hard or soft, heavy or light, hot or cold. A fuzzy blanket is soft. A bicycle helmet is hard.

Color is another physical property of matter. Matter comes in all kinds of colors. The ocean can be blue or green. The sun is yellow. You can see through some matter, like glass and water.

Properties of Matter

hot

a bowl of hot soup

cold

an igloo

hard

a cement block

soft

ducklings

smooth

a dolphin

rough

tree bark

A diamond is one of the hardest natural materials on Earth.

19

Density and Volume

All matter has mass. Mass is the amount of matter inside an object. Objects with more mass have more density. A bowling ball has more mass than a beach ball. It's denser. Oil is less dense than water. That's why oil floats on water.

Volume is the space that matter takes up. Solids and liquids always keep the same volume when put into containers. Gas spreads out to fill whatever container it is in. Its volume changes. When you blow up a balloon, your breath fills the whole balloon.

A solid's volume is usually measured by units such as cubic centimeters (cm^3).

Mass and Weight

Weight measures how hard gravity pulls down on an object. Without gravity, everything on Earth would float into space!

Mass is not the same as weight. An object's mass never changes. But its weight might. The pull of gravity is not the same on every planet. If you went to Mars, you would weigh less than you do on Earth. That's because Mars has weaker gravity.

"Remember to look up at the stars and not down at your feet. Try to make sense of what you see and wonder about what makes the universe exist. Be curious."

– physicist Stephen Hawking

The sun's gravity is about 28 times stronger than Earth's gravity. The sun's gravity pulls on Earth. It keeps Earth and the other planets in orbit.

On Earth, a person with a mass of 50 kilograms weighs 110 pounds.

On Mars, a person with a mass of 50 kilograms weighs 42 pounds.

Changing States of Matter

Matter can change states. Have you ever eaten an ice-cream cone on a hot summer day? After a while the ice cream begins to melt. Why? The sun's heat raised the air's temperature. The higher temperature turned the solid ice cream into a liquid.

Not all solids melt. When wood is heated, it turns into ash. This is a chemical change. It can't be changed back.

Some matter changes states when heat is added or taken away. Add heat to water. Eventually it boils. Some boiling water escapes into the air as a gas. This is called steam.

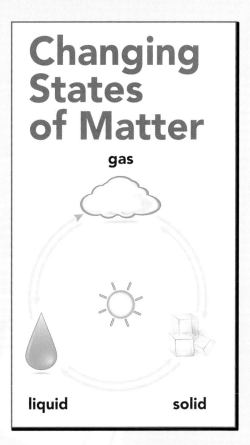

Changing States of Matter

gas

liquid   solid

Melting Points of Solids

chocolate	97 degrees Fahrenheit (36 degrees Celsius)
gold	1,943 degrees F (1,062 degrees C)
iron	2,750 degrees F (1,510 degrees C)

Boiling Points of Liquids

water at sea level	212 degrees F (100 degrees C)
household vinegar	213 degrees F (101 degrees C)
olive oil	572 degrees F (300 degrees C)

The Water Cycle

Rain and snow depend on the changing states of matter. For rain to form, the air fills with water vapor. The water vapor rises and cools. Then it turns into water droplets. It has changed from a gas into a liquid. The droplets form clouds in the sky. Sometimes the droplets are heavier than air. When this happens, they fall from the sky as raindrops.

Dew forms on grass when water vapor in the air loses heat.

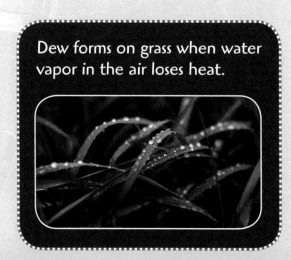

Water Cycle

droplets are
heavier than air

clouds form

rain or
snow falls

water
vapor rises

water collects
on the ground

Mixing Matter

Matter doesn't just change. It can be mixed together. Take a glass of water and some ice cubes. The solid ice cube melts into the liquid water. This causes the water to cool. The ocean is made of salt water. Salt is a solid. The salt dissolves into the ocean water, creating saltwater.

Matter matters! It is all around you. Step outside and look up. The sun and clouds are made of matter. Now look down. The ants crawling along the sidewalk are made of matter. So is the sidewalk. There would be no life on Earth without matter.

Glossary

atom (AT-uhm)—the smallest part of matter

density (DEN-si-tee)—the amount of mass an object or substance has based on a unit of volume

gravity (GRAV-uh-tee)—a force that pulls objects together

mass (MASS)—the amount of material in an object

microscope (MYE-kruh-skope)—a tool that makes very small things look large enough to be seen

orbit (OR-bit)—the path an object such as a planet follows as it goes around the sun

oxygen (OK-suh-juhn)—a colorless gas that people and animals breathe; humans and animals need oxygen to live

property (PROP-ur-tee)—quality in a material, such as color, hardness, or shape

trillion (TIL-yuhn)—1,000 times one billion

volume (VOL-yuhm)—the amount of space taken up by an object or substance

water vapor (WAH-tur VY-pur)—water in gas form; water vapor is one of many invisible gases in the air

weight (WATE)—a measurement of how heavy something is

Critical Thinking Questions

1. What are three states of matter?

2. Every object has mass and weight. Why is an object's weight greater on Earth than on Mars?

3. On cold days, your breath looks like a white cloud. What is happening to your breath?

Read More

Diehn, Andi. *Matter: Physical Science for Kids.* Physical Science for Kids. White River Junction, VT: Nomad Press, 2018.

Dunne, Abbie. *Matter.* Physical Science. North Mankato, MN: Capstone Press, 2017.

Squire, Ann O. *Matter.* A True Book. New York: Children's Press, 2019.

Internet Sites

States of Matter
http://www.chem4kids.com/files/matter_states.html

DK Find Out. States of Matter.
https://www.dkfindout.com/us/science/solids-liquids-and-gases/states-matter/

Index